TIME CHASERS

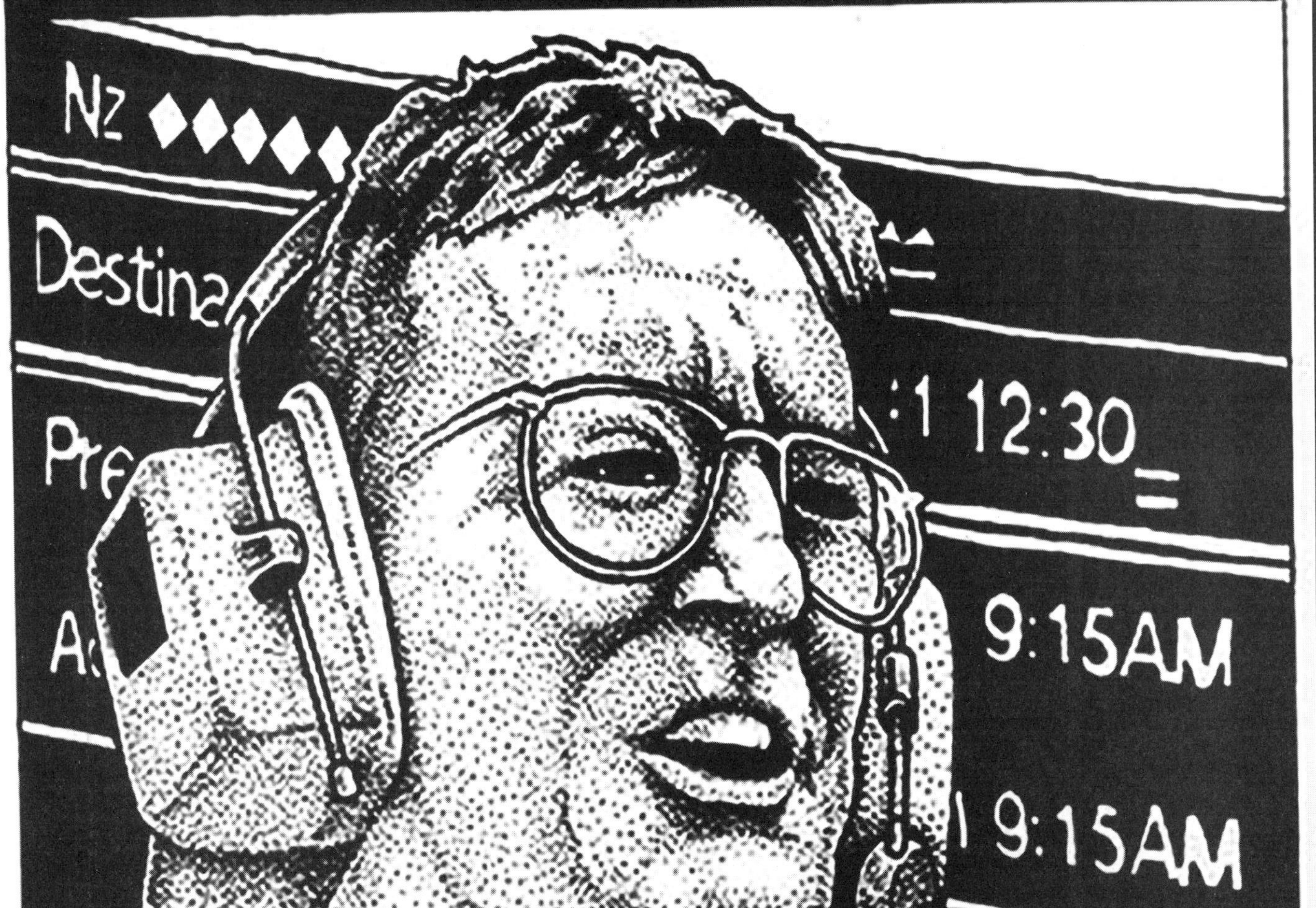

TIME CHASERS:

THE COLORING BOOK

A RIFFTRAX EXCLUSIVE

BY:

JORDAN R. COLTON

COVER BY:

PATRICK KENDALL

RIFFTRAX EVENTS!!!

RIFFTRAX LIVE!

TIME CHASERS

THURSDAY, MAY 5TH

IN HUNDREDS OF THEATERS NATIONWIDE

ENCORE ON MAY 17TH!

LEARN MORE @ RIFFTRAX.COM/TIMECHASERS

COLORING CONTEST! COLOR THESE PAGES AND POST ONLINE WITH #RIFFTRAXLIVE TO WIN COOL RIFFTRAX SWAG

DEDICATION

This is dedicated to Rifftrax, and all the kickstarter supporters!
Thank you!

```
V K X D J M J A G R M S D M B A O U K O
I P E R P O A N G A M R A O B L I L F C
I Y P V R W X E R U A G N U I O P H P O
G Y C W I Y A Y M D Z N D D L C Q N C B
P M R F X N J W O Z I Y S F L N O P X L
Q G S C S O M O C E C Q N Y C A D B W A
S N A E P Y W U P O Q Y A K O I D P S K
J R O E L E U R R U X O A L R G C T T P
Q I H S G N I D X P E F O J B D S D F E
E L I R L T N E A T H Q S V E I G N E H
J W O N C E M N P A G Y P L T V L E N Y
I E K H G N N P D A U H V T T A I U H T
G M A B L R P L E U T I H F H D Q M A Y
T R B M A T T H E W B R U C H T U H K X
D N O T G N I R R A H R E T E P S Q F G
R C J Q L E B W Z F H F X R D U I Y P R
E I G Q P I L P K D W C F F Z T O J E F
E V G T H I I E M V S M I H I W N G R L
F F W U Q W M N Y L I M V M U M T A O M
D B V Q W N V Y J E X X J T T U L O E Z
```

BILL CORBETT   BONNIE PRITCHARD   DAVID GIANCOLA   GEORGE WOODARD

KEVIN MURPHY   MARY JO PEHL   MATTHEW BRUCH   MICHAEL NELSON

PETER HARRINGTON

Jordan Colton Presents

An Edgewood Studios Production

A Horrid Coloring Book:

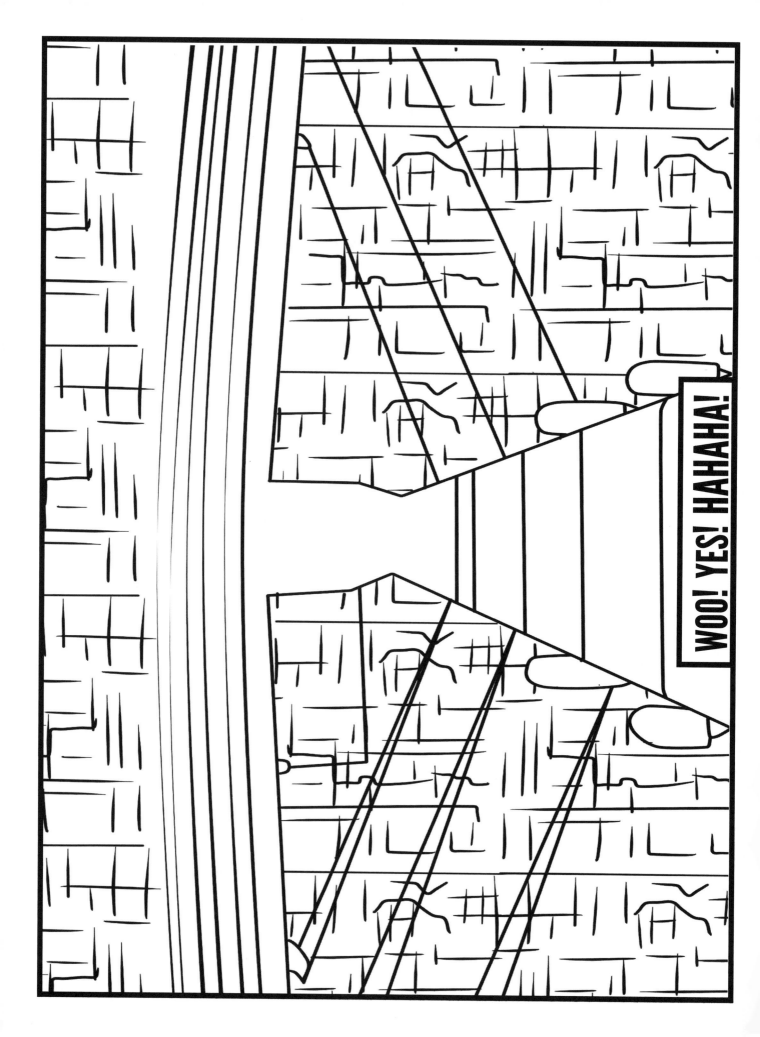

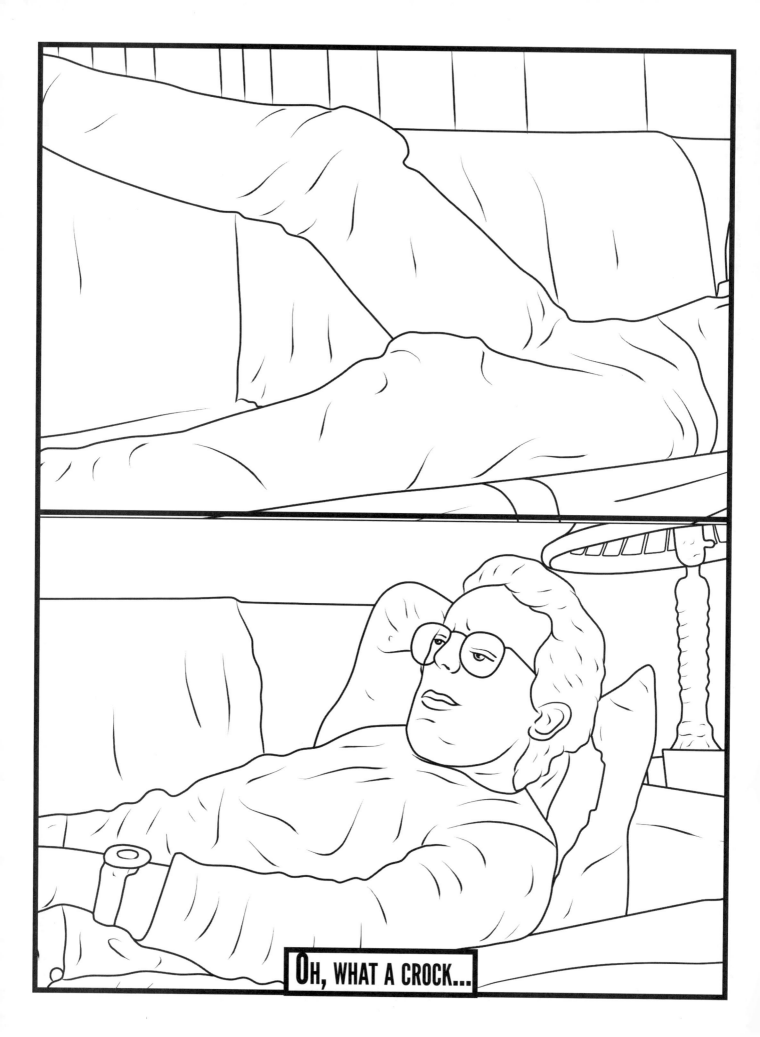

Nick Explains How Simple Time Travel Works:

You see, This PC is connected to a series of molecule accelerators that are attached to the skin of the plane. The computer runs a series of equations in about 8 picoseconds. Obviously, I had to speed up the computer's RAM quite a bit for that. Anyway, the computer signals the molecule accelerators, which in turn, charge the skin of the plane, which enables anyone within the inside of the skin of the plane to travel through the passage of time. Now the longer it's charged, the further you can go into the future. And of course I can reverse the polarity and go back in time as well. Got it?

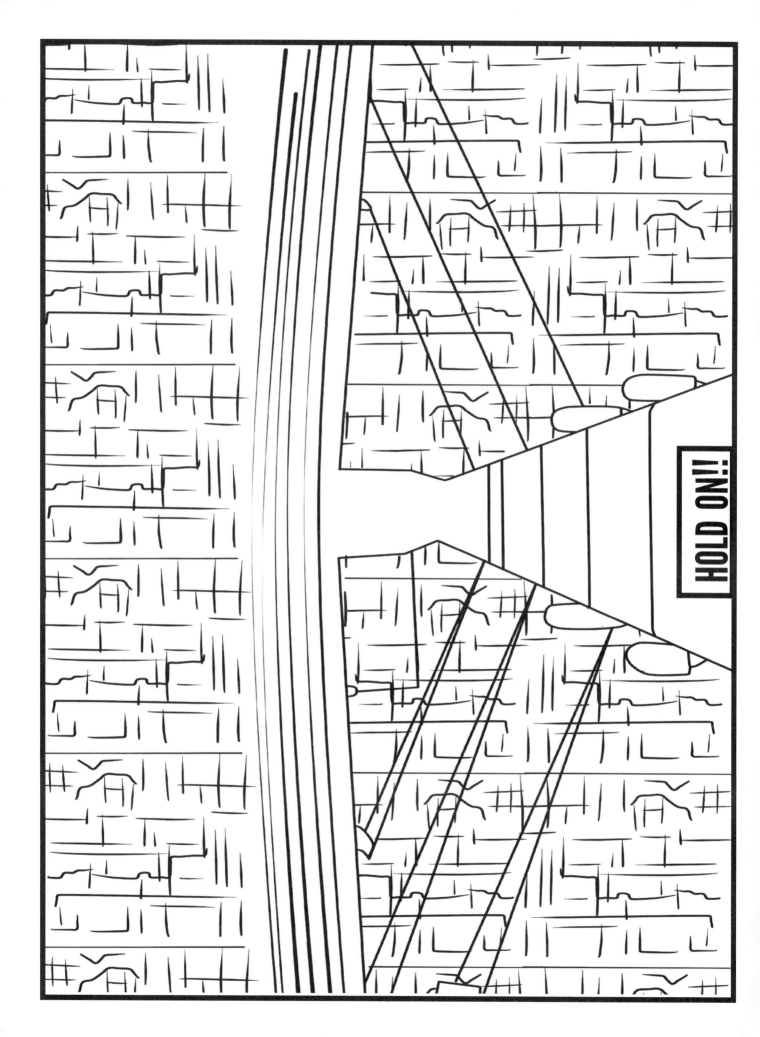

EVERYONE, THIS IS AN AUSPICIOUS DAY IN THE HISTORY OF THE WORLD.

HELP NICK AND LISA FIND THE HOBO AND SAFETY

HELP NICK AND LISA ESCAPE GEN-CORP!

ELEVATOR

EXIT

"ANY SURVIVORS?" "YOU KIDDING? WE'LL BE LUCKY TO FIND DENTAL RECORDS."

MY PLANE....WE NEED TO TAKE A LITTLE TRIP.

WITH SO MANY "NICKS" FROM DIFFERENT TIME SPLITS CAN YOU SPOT THE DIFFERENT "NICK" BELOW? (HINT: THEY ALL HAVE THE SAME CHIN AND MULLET)

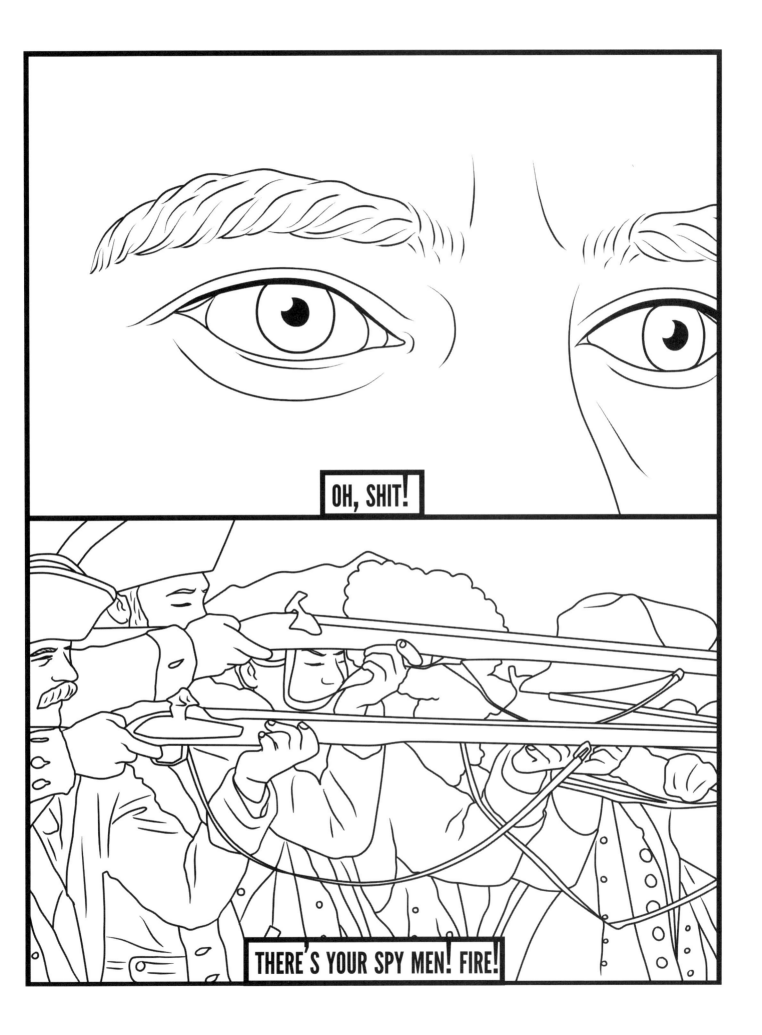

Delete Transport Program Disk 7B
Disk 7B Deleted

Delete Transport Program Disk 8B
Are you sure? This is the LAST program disk
Yes

THE END

ABOUT THE AUTHOR

Jordan Colton is an avid fan of horror & bad movies. He currently resides in Utah with his cat and horror film collection.

You can learn more about his coloring books at:
www.horridcoloringbooks.com

Use the promo code "castleton" for free shipping in the US.

Also check out his other coloring books:

Volume 1: The Night of the Living Dead

Volume 2: The Krampus

Volume 3: Manos the Hands of Fate

Follow Patrick Kendall at "The Mordacious Art of Patrick Kendall" on Facebook

Find out more about "Time Chasers "at
EdgewoodStudios.com